WOMEN who Boss Up

SPECIAL EDITION

WOMEN who Boss Up

TODAY IS THE FIRST DAY OF THE REST OF YOUR LIFE

LORI PFEIFER MURPHY

Copyright © 2025 by Lori Pfeifer Murphy

All rights reserved. This book or any portion thereof may not be reproduced or used in any manner whatsoever without the express written permission of the publisher except for the use of brief quotations in a book review.

First Printing, 2025

Cover Design by Bojan Reković
Book Interior Design by VMC Art & Design, LLC

ISBN: 979-8-9885681-4-8
Library of Congress Control Number: 1-15031663051

Delucslife Media, LLC
30 N Gould Sheridan Wyoming 82801

Printed in USA

PUBLISHER'S MESSAGE

WE BELIEVE IN THE POWER OF PERSONAL GROWTH—and the bravery it takes to follow your inner calling, even when the path ahead is unclear. Lori Pfeifer Murphy's story is a beautiful reminder that it's never too late to become who you were always meant to be.

Today is the First Day of the Rest of Your Life isn't just a title—it's a powerful statement. It reflects Lori's inspiring journey, from her roots in the beauty industry to finding her stride in real estate, and from quietly dreaming of writing to courageously stepping into her role as an author. Her path is filled with divine timing, surprising mentors, and meaningful moments that came from simply choosing to say "yes."

In this book, Lori invites us into a deeply personal space—where transformation is driven by faith, gratitude, and purpose. What started as a spark of inspiration, fueled by the bold stories of other women, became a full-circle moment shaped by mentorship, sisterhood, and a calling to lift others up. Through her words, we're reminded that sometimes, all it takes is one choice, one person, or one moment to shift everything.

We're honored to walk alongside Lori in this debut. Her voice is genuine, her story is timely, and her heart shines through every page. Whether you're navigating change, searching for your next step, or simply need a reminder that you're not alone—this book will meet you where you are.

May Lori's journey remind you that nothing in life is random—the people, the paths, and the passions are all part of something greater. And may you feel the same grace, courage, and hope that lives within these pages.

Because truly—right now—is the first day of the rest of your life.

"Today is the First Day of the Rest of Your Life"

A FAVORITE SAYING OF MY GRANDPA'S THAT HAS COME to shape how I live.

At first, I thought they were just words, simple and ordinary. But as I've lived my life, I've come to understand their meaning more deeply. They remind me that each day is a chance to begin again, to grow, to keep going.

This is my Grandma and Grandpa, two people who meant the

world to me. Though they lived in Memphis and I was in Ohio, we were close. I saw them often, and each moment with them left a lasting mark on my heart.

They taught me, through their faith in God, that love isn't just something you say but it's something you do. They prayed for me, cared for me, and showed up in quiet, consistent ways that spoke louder than words. Their love was steady, real, and full of grace and I am deeply grateful for that.

They always believed in me, even when I didn't believe in myself. Their love was constant, their prayers unceasing, and their faith in me never wavered. So much of who I am today was shaped by their presence in my life.

I carry their memory with me every day, with gratitude, with love, and with the quiet strength they helped instill in me.

With love and memory,
Lori Pfeifer Murphy
For Grandma and Grandpa

PREFACE

I'VE WANTED TO WRITE A BOOK FOR AS LONG AS I CAN remember. Decisions you make in your life will put you into situations that can allow things to just fall into place. That's how I came to write this book.

I had been in the beauty industry for most of my career until about 4 years ago. Due to the circumstances I was in, I joined a real estate company that led me to meet some very influential people in my life. I went to a seminar in Orlando and to the stage came Rebecca and Jose Soto, a power couple to say the least. They run a brokerage in Orlando, are married, have children, and have written a book together. From the moment Rebecca started to speak, I knew I had to meet her. She was dynamic! Besides the fact of being stunningly beautiful, she owned the stage. She was what I wanted to become. She has a presence about her that demands attention, but in a loving, sweet, and authentic way. She knew her business too, you could easily see how she and her husband had become so successful.

I got back home and looked her up on social media. I messaged her and low and behold, she answered me. We scheduled a call to talk and get to know each other. Instantly, we were friends! She was in the process of being a part of a book, *Women Who Boss Up in Real Estate*. There were 15 other women in the book with her. I was intrigued, but had just begun my start in real estate and thought I had nothing to write about.

Fast forward to last October when I got my broker license. I reached out again to Rebecca and asked her about the book she had written. How could I become involved? I had always wanted to write a book, maybe I could start by being in a book with other women who had similar interests as me. She introduced me to Tam Luc. Tam is the founder of Women Who Boss Up, an organization that supports women and their businesses through marketing. Tam and I grew up 15 minutes from each other in Ohio! She was from Forest Park and I was from Fairfield. We are the same age with similar backgrounds in the beauty industry. Fate had brought us together.

Over the past 8 months, she has become my mentor. She has inspired me to write this book. We were originally going to be a part of a book together with 15 other women, but through the process, she decided for us to each write our own book. She has coached us throughout the whole process. We had a retreat here in Fort Pierce, where I currently live. She took us through different exercises that inspired the words to follow in this book.

I wanted to write this part of the book to give me a chance to say thank you. Thank you, Rebecca, for being such an inspiration and friend. Thank you, Tam, for being the mentor I needed in my life at the time I needed it.

Thank you, God, for loving me and showing me the grace and courage I've needed throughout my life. Thank you for never leaving my side. You are my rock! You are my source! You are my friend! You are all that I need! I love you!

Thank you to my children, Chelsey, Jake, and Troy. You have

inspired me in my life more than you could ever imagine. You are the strength that carries me through each day. You are my "why" I do what I do. I am so proud of you!! Momma loves you very much!!!

Thank you to my Mom and Dad for always believing in me. I love you!

Thank you to my husband for always supporting me. You are my best friend, I love you.

"Energy flows where focus goes."

—*Tony Robbins*

CHAPTER 1

Foundations of Success: Gratitude and Prayer

WHY SHOULD YOU BEGIN EACH DAY WITH GRATITUDE? We need to understand the true meaning of gratitude and how it will affect your life. Gratitude has three parts. First: feeling grateful for the good things that you have in your life. Second: expressing your gratitude to the people who have made your life better, and third: adopting new behaviors as a result of interacting with those who have helped you. I like to begin each day with a moment of gratitude. You cannot be both grateful and upset at the same time. It is physically and mentally impossible. Gratitude brings appreciation. You don't take things for granted when you are appreciating what you have instead of what you may not. This allows you to begin your day in a mindset of gratitude.

When you are in control of your mindset, or your state of mind, you allow yourself the ability to choose what will affect your day and how it will affect your day. For me, I begin my day in the Word. I am thankful for God. I am thankful for all of the things He allows me to have in my life. This will ensure I begin each day with a smile. Once you fill your mind and heart with goodness, it should flow out of you throughout the day. People will say, "my heart was in it," and that's great, but what did your mouth and actions show? The more you fill your mind and spirit with things that are good, the more it will become a habit to act and speak things that are good.

The Pike Place Market in Seattle, Washington has a theory, "The Fish Philosophy". I love this because it speaks to this very point. Think about working at a fish market; the smell, the atmosphere, probably wet, maybe dreary. **The Pike Place Market** makes a point to find the good in their surroundings. Number 1: Have Fun! I love this! Have fun while you're selling (or throwing) fish! Their philosophy is to make it fun! It's your job which means you're probably there more than you are at your home, make it fun! They throw the fish to their customers. Laughing, singing, yelling, and making a commotion to get by-stander's attention. Which in turn brings more business. I know whether I wanted fish or not, I would buy one to be able to play! I worked in Research and Development at Procter and Gamble and I was fortunate enough that my director allowed me to decorate our conference room. I made each wall a different color, we had an 80" TV hung on the back wall for meetings and "Movie Afternoons". We also began a new tradition of "Smoothie Fridays." Our walls could become very serious and mundane, but this conference room allowed everyone an opportunity to have fun and bring some color and excitement into our world. I may not have been able to do it had we not been working on "Herbal Essences", but fortunately we were.

Number 2: Choose Your Attitude. This is one of my favorites! You have the authority to choose your attitude everyday in every situation. You are not in control of what you may be faced with each day, but you are in control of how you respond. It's not about the things that happen to you, but how you choose to respond to those things. This is an on-going challenge, of course, but the more you are aware of your attitude, I feel as though you will make better choices. When I worked at Ulta Beauty as a Salon Manager, I would urge my stylists to be very aware of their attitude when they approached their client. Smile, look them in the eye, truly listen to what they have to say. They are paying for your expertise and time. Make it worth it. If you had a bad morning, someone cut you off on the way into work, no one needs to know about it! Leave it at the door, trust me it will still be there after your shift, but you may not care about it as much.

Number 3: Be There. Be present in each moment. How often have you been in a conversation with someone and you know they are already thinking of how they will respond to you? You haven't even finished your thought and they are already down a different path. Being present means you take the time to listen. Take in your surroundings. Appreciate each moment. I always say I do not want to be the smartest person in the room. I can always learn from others. Be there. Be present. We went out to dinner last weekend and I looked around at the tables and noticed something very disturbing. Everyone was on their phone. There were minimal conversations happening at the tables. What could be so important that you can't put your phone away for an hour to spend time with loved ones? One thing I loved about visiting my grandparents in Memphis was they hardly ever had the TV on when they had company. We would all sit together in the family room, Grandpa would make a fire if it was cold, and we would talk about what was happening in our lives. Everyone would be engaged and involved in the conversations. Laughing and making memories. I remember my daughter took her first steps in that family room, we may have missed it if the TV was on! It is so important to be present in each moment. One thing we will never get back is our time. I try to do my best to cherish it!

Finally, number 4: Make Someone's Day! This statement means a lot to me on many levels. I worked for Aveda for many years of my adult life. David Wagner, owner of JUUT salons, wrote a book called *The Daymaker*. The storyline of the book is that you never know what people are going through in their lives and how you can touch them. David speaks of being in the salon and at the end of a long shift a woman walks in for a last minute style. He was tired from his day and really just wanted to go home, but he agreed to stay. He treated her as he did every guest, beginning with a stress relieving treatment, hand massage, and a make up finishing touch before she left. As he was checking her out, he noticed a tear running down her cheek. He asked if she liked her hair, was there anything else he could do for her? She said, "everything was great, in fact better than I could have imagined. The truth is, I came in to have my hair done today because I was planning to kill myself. You made me feel so special and so important, that you actually made me realize, I do matter. I am important. Thank you." Be a Daymaker!

As I think about gratitude, I can't help but go to prayer. God is my center, my creator, and the source of all that I am. Beginning each day with prayer allows me to focus on "The Word" versus "The World". Psalm 23, a very familiar verse to most people, hit me like a ton of bricks a few weeks ago. Each morning, I like to do Bible roulette. I open the Bible randomly to a verse that I feel God wants to speak to me through. This particular morning I opened to Psalm 23. "The Lord is my shepherd, I shall not want….." If you don't know the verse, please look it up! This verse has been said and even sung in many churches, but mostly I've heard it at funerals. I thought it was more about death, but on this particular morning, God spoke to me in a way that changed my perspective on this verse. If you think about a shepherd herding their sheep, if one sheep roams away, what does the shepherd do? He leaves the pack to go and find that one sheep! Throughout my life, even throughout any given day, I find myself feeling insecure for different reasons. What this verse says to me is that He will never let me stray. He will never leave me. Even if I walk away, He is close by. As I look back on my life, the times of joy and peace, I had God as my focus. This verse takes away my fears and brings me comfort in knowing my God is always by my side.

The world will bring many challenges for me to face, but the Word will arm me with the right protection and armor I need to make it through each day. This is a work in progress. I still struggle at times with insecurity, but the more you practice at something, the better you become. I practice in the Word each day and each day I become stronger. If you've never read the Bible, it can feel intimidating. I have the New Living Translation Bible. It's written in a way that I can relate to and understand. I take notes in church on Sunday and then that is my guide to reading throughout the week. I've not read it from beginning to end, but hopefully by the end of my time I would have. I like Bible roulette because it allows God to show me what he wants me to read each day. I'm always pleasantly surprised by what he puts in front of me!

Preparation is key to success. Michael Jordan did not become the greatest to ever play the game of basketball by not practicing and preparing for that success. What pain are you willing to endure in order to achieve the ultimate success? Late nights? Rejection? Physical and emotional tolls? Darren Hardy said, "It's not just about the heights, but it's about the depths." You cannot achieve the height without digging deep into the depths. Don't focus on the end result and miss the journey.

I used to do hair for weddings. The commotion within the hotel suite was intense. Just imagine 5-6 bridesmaids, flower girl, mother-of-the-bride, mother-of-the-groom, maybe a couple of grandmas, a big spread of food, champagne, the wedding dress, the bridesmaids dresses, all the stuff! I was in one corner flinging hair and my friend, Andriana, in the other corner perfecting their beauty with makeup. The music is blaring in the background, laughter and tears from all. Sometimes, even a few heated moments. The bride on her phone; are the flowers here, is the cake here, are the chairs set up on the beach, did my fiancé make it to the hotel, etc… I was usually the last to have the bride before the big reveal. There is so much happening around her during this time. We've probably already been there for 4-5 hours. When we began everyone was taking pictures, but now the bridesmaids have their hair and make up finished, they are busy getting dressed.

So many times, I had to remind them to take pictures of their "best friend," the bride. Why were they all there at this moment! So much commotion, so much estrogen in one room! It can be easy to miss the moment of the journey. I would always remind the bride to stop, take a look around, and enjoy the moment. She is in the room with her very best friends, her mom, maybe grandma, the room is filled with so much love. There is so much that has to happen to get to this very moment. Don't miss it! Sometimes we focus so much on the end result that we miss the journey that got us there. At a wedding there may not be many of life's lessons, but the idea is the same. Proper planning and preparation by all is what makes it a success. The caterer, the hairdresser, the make up artist, the musicians, the pastor, florist, the decorator, the wedding planner, the photographer, the venue caretaker, and the fashion designer of the wedding dress. All of this planning and preparation and training that goes into a wedding. How much more prepared must you be for your day!!!

Winning is what happens before the game! I make a lot of sports references. I grew up in Ohio. In the winter there wasn't much else to do but watch football. I remember growing up in Chardon and my dad would watch the Browns on Sundays. If you know anything about football and the Browns you know they don't win very much. But, we keep believing they will one day! I love the game of football. The quarterback gets a lot of the praise because he is involved in most of the plays, but just as in business, the quarterback couldn't be successful without those around him. The lineman protects him from the defenders who are trying to smear him all over the turf. The center hikes him the ball. The running back takes the ball to the endzone. The tight end or the receiver catches the ball for a touchdown and the kicker kicks the extra point! On the back end you have numerous coaches studying the other teams offense and defense in order to be the best equipped for the game on Sunday.

During the week: workouts, studying films, eating right, DR visits, practices, learning new plays, all while living a balanced life. Their work and dedication goes into entertaining millions on Sundays! During high school I was a football trainer. I saw those boys work to the point of complete exhaustion in hopes to see the field on Friday night. Tom Brady recently gave a speech where he said: "Everyone should play football. Why? Because it's hard." It will prepare you for hard things in your life. This statement is so very true. Life is hard and the way you prepare yourself will determine your success.

"Patience and perseverance have a magical effect before which difficulties disappear and obstacles vanish."

—John Quincy Adams

CHAPTER 2

The Waiting Game: Cultivating Patience in a Fast-Paced Market

PATIENCE SEEMS TO GET A BAD RAP. I THINK PATIENCE can be an asset when used correctly in your daily practices. The ability to have patience when approached with a decision allows you the opportunity to sit back and review all of the different options and their potential outcomes. Have you ever played a game of chess? The best chess players are thinking 3-4 moves ahead, already anticipating the different outcomes. The art of negotiating is based on your ability to be patient.

"The trick in investing is just to sit there and watch pitch after pitch go by and wait for the one right in your sweet spot." - Warren Buffett

The definition of perseverance according to Webster's Dictionary is: "continued effort to do or achieve something despite difficulties, failure, or opposition."

I began my career in cosmetology. It took me 5 years to get my license. I began cosmetology school right out of high school at 18 years old, but during that time got pregnant with my daughter, Chelsey. My focus had to change to take care of her. I had to step away from school for a while. I knew I would finish, but the timing was unclear. Two years later, I was able to complete my hours and pass my test! At this point, I was pregnant with my son, Jake. Once licensed, I began my career in an Aveda salon: Shear Genius. I was an assistant; washing hair, rinsing perms, sweeping hair, washing and folding towels, getting water or tea for the clients, and anything else that was asked of me. Aveda had a distributorship in the town where I lived, Fairfield, Ohio. I enjoyed doing hair and being with the clients, but I felt the need for more. I wanted to explore other options within the industry.

I was fortunate to get a job at the distributorship, Aveda Fredrics, as an Account Executive. I was thrilled. I was working with salons in the area to reach their goals through merchandising, retail, and educating the stylists on how to achieve higher ticket amounts which equates to higher take home pay. By this time, I was married and pregnant with another child, my youngest son, Troy. Aveda opened an institute in the area and I was offered an instructor position. I accepted. As I reflect back on all I've done throughout my career, teaching others is by far my biggest joy! Seeing the light bulb go off in someone's head is the biggest rush of dopamine. My days were filled with educating and being educated.

Fast forward to 2016, I moved to Florida to be the assistant director at the Aveda Institute in Davie. My role was to assist the Director in the day to day duties of reaching our goals, but also to assist with the students and make their experience the best I could as we prepared them for a career in beauty. I embraced this role like I had never done before. I moved to Florida by myself, not knowing anyone. It was a little scary, but I used that emotion to push me forward. I was too excited to be scared. I've heard being scared and excited are the same reaction for your physiological self, it's how you choose to feel it. I chose excitement!

As the assistant director, I was employed to assist the director, but also to engage the students to a deeper educational experience. I embraced this role! I would come in early and stay late. We partnered with the local chamber of commerce. This allowed the students the opportunity to be involved in the community. We also participated in the Joe DiMaggio foundation dance. The students were able to do the hair and make up for the patients. This was an experience that I hope stayed with them. It's a thrill to do what you love and at the same time brighten someone's day! We had a partnership with the Miami Dolphin cheerleaders where we would do their hair for special events and in turn we would be on the jumbo-tron after each quarter. My personal favorite perk was the tickets to the games!! Yes, I was at the games!! Big win!

Each week we had a pep rally where all of the students would meet on the floor for upcoming events, education on new products or services, and we would bring in guests to present. I loved this time and tried to make it as fun as possible for the students. We had karaoke contests, hula hoop contests, trivia days, anything to hold their attention.

Camp Aveda was held the first week of the students' start of school. Day 3 was all about Wellness: health, financial, spiritual, mental, intellectual, and physical. We would begin the day with yoga and end with a spiritual walk in the garden. Needless to say, I was in my element.

The assistant director position was being eliminated. Some were let go, but I was offered the opportunity to move into the Admission's role. This was the bread and butter of the institute. Our return on investment. At the time, I saw it as a demotion. I wanted to be the Director. I wanted to continue to do all of the things I had put into place. Do you notice the trend here? I, I, I! It wasn't until I was preparing this book that I finally admitted to myself that instead of seeing this as a demotion, I needed to see it as a true compliment to what I had to offer the Institute. They put me in the position to be the first person a potential student would see and meet when choosing to sign up and pay for their education. I was in my own way! If I would have taken a step back and was patient to see the "why" behind the change in my role, we may have had another ending to my story. I do believe that everything happens for a reason, but I also believe sometimes we can make it much more difficult on ourselves by the decisions we make. Another topic we will touch on later in this book.

Eventually, my lack of interest in my new role got me fired! A big piece of humble pie!

Fortunately for me, I was known for my successes in my role and not my final act of selfishness.

The Salon People, the Aveda distributor in Florida, had another side of the business apart from the Institutes; the salon side. The role was similar to what I held in Ohio. I was hired to service the salons in Jacksonville and then later South Florida. I was happy. I was learning and working with salons again. Educating on the products, technical skills, and living my best life. I appreciated the fact I was given another chance. My role was to help the current salons, but also to open new Aveda salons. I was given the opportunity to work with the very best in the business.

Learning never ends! I embraced the opportunities I was given. I remember facilitating a class for a salon in Boca Raton, Dorjon Salon. I was presenting the 5 C's of the salon experience. I won't bore you with the details, but during this time I remember being so happy. I was improving their clients' experience as well as showing them ways to increase their income. Life was good. I went in early and stayed late. Time had no measurement to me, when you're doing something you love, it never seems like work; I was living my passion.

March 2020: COVID! The moment the world stopped. The salon world was paused. We continued to work very closely with our salon owners, helping them apply and receive PPP during this time. We had daily Zoom calls (looking back, we all should have bought stock in Zoom). Tom, the owner of The Salon People, did all he could to keep all of us financially healthy, but the dreaded day came. I got a Facetime call from Tom. I will never forget seeing his name pop up on my phone. I was thrilled he was reaching out to me. He would check in from time to time. He was very involved with all of his employees, we were like family. Once I saw his face, I knew it was not just a "checking in" phone call. The PPP had run out and he was forced to make decisions that would impact some of the people on his team. I was one of those people.

At that moment, my world came crashing down. I remember trying to hold back the tears, I needed to be strong, but I broke down. I cried. Big girl tears, I cried.

My whole identity was Aveda and the beauty industry. This was all I had ever done. I was good at it. What was I going to do now? Fortunately, I was given some capital to make it for a small while, but I needed to decide what my next steps were going to be. Do I go back to Ohio?

By this time, I was married to Todd. He owned half of a real estate company and a title company. He offered for me to help out at the title company while I figured out what I wanted to do next. I didn't want to go work for a salon, it was during COVID. I took a step back and decided it was time to move forward. My role in the salon industry was finished.

Now, I could have curled up into a ball and fallen victim to my circumstances, but that is not Lori! I will not fail. I will survive.

I began working at the title company and to my surprise, I really liked it. I'm a huge fan of black and white structure. Title is definitely black and white. I've always loved to help people, and what better way than to help them with one of the biggest financial decisions of their life. Todd suggested I get my real estate license, so I did. Todd suggested I get my title license, so I did. Todd suggested I get my Broker license, so I did. Three not very easy licenses to get, but I got them all within 3 years. Not bad.

When I began my career journey, I was a cosmetologist. I still have that license today, but my experiences equipped me with the confidence to strive forward and be able to achieve more than I thought possible. I'm not finished yet! A little patience and belief in yourself, with the right opportunities can open many doors you never thought possible.

Perseverance: Continued effort to do or achieve something despite difficulties, failure or opposition.

My identity was the beauty industry, now my identity is **ME.**

"But the Lord said to Samuel, "Don't judge by his appearance or height, for I have reflected him. The Lord doesn't make decisions the way you do! People judge by outward appearance, but the Lord looks at a person's thoughts and intentions.""

—1 Samuel 16:7

CHAPTER 3

Mirror Moments: The Power of Self-Reflection for Growth

HOW DOES SELF-REFLECTION LEAD TO CHANGE IN your life? Why is it so important to love ourselves before loving others? Do you take full responsibility for your actions? Are you able to apologize?

My mom and dad got divorced when I was 15 years old. My brother moved away to college in Michigan shortly after. I chose to live with my dad. He traveled a lot for work which left me at home to take care of myself. My mom lived close by for about a year and then moved to Memphis to be closer to my grandparents.

It was a cold winter morning, and I was warm in my water bed (we had those back in the 80s). The thought of walking from my room to the bathroom to shower was not at all what I wanted to do. My dad was out of town for work, my mom lived elsewhere. Did I have to get up? No one was there to say. Now, I knew I was supposed to be at school in less than an hour, but my bed was so warm and cozy. I called the school's phone number, Mrs. Blum answered. I told her that our toilet had overflowed and my dad was out of town. BINGO! I was in bed for another 2 hours!

Looking back, I actually made this decision more than I should have. In fact, if you were late more than 10 times in a class, you failed. Needless to say, I failed my 1st period that quarter. Maybe I acted as any teenager would who didn't have supervision at home. Maybe I acted better than other teenagers would who didn't have any supervision at home. All I know is, looking back, I wish I would've taken responsibility for my education. I wish I would have had more direction and goals that I wanted to achieve. I don't regret my past because it's how I became who I am today, but you can't help but wonder what might have been. I spent many years blaming the situation (my parents divorce) for my actions, but it was not the situation. It was not my parent's fault that I didn't try harder, it was my choices. Everyday, you wake up with a choice to get up or lay in bed. Today, I try much harder to get up!

I became a mom at 19 years old. Most of my friends were going off to college, frat parties, football games, studying with friends, and all the things most do at 19 years of age. My decisions gave me a child. Late night feedings, changing diapers, cleaning up spit up off of every shirt I owned. But, this was my choice. The consequences for my actions changed the direction of my life. I have no regrets, I love my daughter very much, but my life did change significantly.

Very soon after Chelsey was born, I was a single mother. I had to support her and myself. As I've told you, I hadn't finished my cosmetology school yet. I worked with a local company that just barely paid the bills. If you ever need to know how many different ways there are to eat potatoes, I'm your girl! I had to make sure Chelsey had her food so for myself, I could afford a bag of potatoes. Enough for a week's worth of dinners for me!

It was a cold November evening in Ohio and the roads were covered with snow. Chelsey and I were driving home after I had picked her up from daycare. We were about 1/4 mile from home and all of a sudden the car began to jerk like it was going to stop. I ran out of gas….why was I surprised? I barely had enough money to live let alone putting gas in the car. I sat for a minute and then grabbed Chelsey in my arms and walked through the snow to our apartment. Chelsey was only 10 months old. She didn't understand. She was happy to be home and in her bed. I remember sitting on the couch and crying. Why me? The answer to that question is easy; the choices you make will determine your outcome. Up until this point, I had not made the best long term choices. If I could speak to my younger self, I would tell her to focus more on the future and how the choices you make can and will affect your future. The next day, I called my dad and he met me at the apartment with a gas can to bring my car home.

You can either sit and weep or you can get up and thrive!

Self reflection is taking a look in the mirror and owning up to your situation. You do not lay blame, justify, or deny the life in front of you. You have to take responsibility. Your current situation is an end result of the decisions you have made up until this point. My choices lead to my current situation.

The Bible verse I wrote at the beginning of this chapter speaks volumes to me now. Most people, including me, spend hours each week maintaining their outward appearances. They should do even more to develop their inner character. While everyone can see your face, only you and God know your thoughts and intentions. Always work to improve your character; your actions are a result of your character.

While working at Ulta Beauty, I was a Salon Market Trainer. We got to go to Chicago each year for a week to learn new ways to go back and train our salon professionals, "Train the Trainer." One year, they brought in a trainer from Canada. He was spectacular. I still use what we learned from him today during speaking engagements. He taught that there are 5 principles to follow when faced with a challenge in life. We used a salon experience, but I like to teach it as a life experience because it fits both. During COVID, I lost my job in the beauty industry. I could have let it defeat me or I could defeat the situation and conquer it. I followed the steps.

Number 1: Take responsibility. Self reflect. Why did I lose my job? Why was I one of the people chosen to be let go? At this point, I had been fired twice in 4 years. Granted, I could not have helped COVID happening in the world, but why was I the one that was let go? One reason I want to write this book and complete this book is because I have had a pattern in my life of not completing things that can be very good for me. Why do I stop? Am I afraid of being successful? There's a book by Gary John Bishop, *UnF*^& Yourself*. This book changed my direction. We tend to go back to a comfort zone subconsciously when we are in situations that are unfamiliar to us. Even if the situation is going to be good for us, our minds can reject it and put us back to where we've been before. For example: If you have always been bad with money and live paycheck to paycheck, if you happen to get a raise and you suddenly have the ability to save money, subconsciously, your actions will spend more to put you back into the "comfort zone" of living paycheck to paycheck. Unless, you are consciously aware and make better decisions. This is why he named the book as he did. Your mind will take you to places of familiarity unless you purposefully don't allow it to. Being purposeful in your thoughts will help you to understand why you will make the decisions you do.

Ultimately, you must take responsibility for your part and take the time to self reflect to better understand the why behind the action. When I was let go from The Salon People because of COVID, I was not let go because of COVID, I was let go because I was not the best on the team. I was replaceable. Once you realize you are replaceable, you either step up or move on. In this situation, I didn't have the opportunity to step up so I made sure my next step would make myself irreplaceable. I got licenses that allow me to work for myself! As an entrepreneur, you are in control of the outcome of your success. You don't have to be at work at any given time, you can watch Netflix all day or scroll through your social media, but your bank account will also reflect how you choose to spend your time. You must be disciplined. You must Boss Up!

Number 2: Be willing. You have to be willing to put the effort, time, energy, and financial responsibility into the next steps you are taking. With my experience, I had to pay for real estate school, which was online because it was during COVID. I had to be disciplined to get up early everyday to study because I had other commitments throughout the day. Learning a new career for 2-3 hours each morning was not easy, but I stayed the course. Learning a new craft online comes with many challenges. You need to find quiet time to focus on the material. No one is telling you a time that you have to be there, you must be disciplined to show up. The only deadline I had was when my subscription would run out. At that point, I could either give up or pay the tuition again. I was not going to do either, so I stuck to the course until I finished.

There were days when "life" got in the way, but that leads me to the next principle.

Number 3: Mistakes are ok. Mistakes are ok as long as they do not continue to happen. Yes, you will have fallbacks, but the important thing is to recognize it and get back on course. If you make a mistake more than twice, it is now a decision. The hardest part about repentance is actually changing your ways. I go back to the Bible a lot because it is my guide in life. Psalm 51:1-12 is the most beautiful prayer of repentance. It not only recognizes the sin (mistake) but David is asking for mercy and guidance to ensure the same mistake doesn't happen again. This is the key to Number 3: Mistakes are ok as long as you own them and they do not continue to happen.

Number 4: Be patient. Change takes time. Change takes repetition. Change takes patience. Surround yourself with the right resources and confidants and you will get to where you need to be. I recommend meditation if you're not good with patience. Meditation allows you to be at one with yourself. Minimal thoughts racing through your head. You take the time to focus on your breathing, your heart beat, how your body feels when remaining very still. Throughout the process of writing this book, meditation became a daily practice. The words would flow onto the paper after times of meditation. Patience is a gift when appreciated.

Finally, number 5: Trust the process. I changed this one to Trust Yourself. You need to believe in yourself. Find a mentor, a coach, a friend who will hold you accountable. My brother, Johnny, is my accountability partner. He may not know this until he reads this book, but there are many times in my life that I will think of him. I respect my brother so much. He has always been very driven. I remember growing up, he never stopped. He was the athlete that would work out all the time. His hard work finally paid off his senior year when he was the wide receiver on the football team and they won the State Championship. I will never forget that feeling. Even as I write now, tears fill my eyes with the joy and excitement of the night. I am so grateful that I was on the field, too. The energy from the full stands at the Ohio State University. Everyone yelling, clapping, and chanting: "FHS FHS FHS!" That team put so much time and effort into becoming champions. Johnny broke records that day! I was so proud, and I am still so proud of my brother.

Fast forward to today, he works just as hard for his family. The drive and commitment he has is very commendable. I'm sure his motivation has changed throughout his life, but failure is not an option. He is my mentor. I stayed with him and his family for almost a year before moving to Florida. I remember a specific afternoon, Johnny and I were talking about my finances and what my next steps would be. I wanted him to be proud of me. He asked me what I was making per year, in order to help me with my budget and I told him more than what it was. When we got to the bottom line number, it didn't add up. He questioned if the figures were correct and I had to tell him that I lied about my income. He said something to me that I will never forget. "Lori, I don't care if you lie to me, but why would you lie to yourself?" This really hit home to me. I wanted him to be proud of me, and I lied because I thought if I made more money it would make a difference. He didn't care about the amount, he cared that I would never get ahead if I couldn't be honest with myself. He cared about me. Be true to yourself. First and foremost. This was a very big lesson for me.

Another time, I called him to discuss business. He is one of the smartest people I know. His business track record is beyond impressive. I remember going to him for advice about a certain situation I was dealing with at work and he told me to read *Start with Why* by Simon Sinek. This book teaches leaders how you can have the greatest influence by how you act, and communicate to those around you. It's all about understanding your "why." I highly recommend it. I believe the more you learn about yourself, the more you will be able to trust yourself to make the best decisions for your life. Surround yourself with good people.

After losing my job from The Salon People, I got my real estate license, title license, and broker license. I took responsibility, was willing to put in the time to get the licenses, and made some mistakes along the way. I was patient, especially with my broker test - third time's a charm! Ultimately, I trusted myself and the process to see it through. Each day, I take time to reflect. What was good today, what can I do better tomorrow? As long as I'm breathing, there is room for improvement.

"Own your morning,
elevate your life."

—Robin Sharma,

author of *The 5 am Club*

"A daily routine built on good habits and disciplines separates the most successful among us from everyone else. The routine is exceptionally powerful."

—*Darren Hardy,*
Author of *The Compound Effect*

CHAPTER 4

Routines that Transform: Daily Practices for Lasting Impact

WHAT ARE YOUR DAILY PRACTICES? EVERYONE HAS A morning routine, does yours set you up for success? Are you living your best life? Your daily routine could make the difference!

The 5 am Club is an excellent read. My son, Jake, bought me this book. It is told as a story, but incorporates best practices that can lead to an elevated life. He speaks of a formula that will allow you to exercise your mind, body, and spirit each day before you ever interact with others. Within the first hour of being awake, you've already read, worked out and took some quiet time to meditate and settle your mind.

I set my alarm each morning for 5 am. The days I don't get up (which are not very many now) are the days that I feel the most weighed down and overwhelmed. It's amazing how your body responds to the options you allow. The days I do get up, I could conquer the world! My routine is as follows: alarm goes off. I do not hit snooze. Snooze is the devil! This allows your brain to think it's ok to remain in bed. In order to have a successful morning routine, you need to eliminate snooze all together. My first 20 minutes or so is in The Word. I play Bible roulette to see what God wants me to read that morning. It's crazy, but it's usually exactly what I needed in my life. I enjoy my time with God. It allows me to be grateful for the things I have in my life. I also ask for guidance and wisdom as I go through my day, remembering to make decisions according to God's will. After I have filled my spirit with The Holy Spirit, it's time to sweat!

My son, Jake, introduced me to CrossFit about 2 years ago. I never thought I would be able to do it. CrossFit is a full body workout with high intensity. When I first went to see Jake in a competition, I was blown away by the determination these athletes have to finish their WODs (Workout of the Day). I'm not as advanced and my workouts are adjusted to fit my level, but it is very rewarding to improve my personal bests. I had no idea how strong I was until I started CrossFit. I love that you work out with others, you're competing to finish a WOD, but it never feels like it's against each other. I remember one of my first WODs, I was pretty far behind everyone, but they came out and ran the last leg with me. I don't think I've ever been in a situation where I was cheered for - it was awesome! If I can't get to the gym, which I try to because working out with others is the best part for me, I will go to our gym and create my own workout utilizing the CrossFit movements. Regardless, you need to move your body for at least 20 minutes each morning. Something to increase your heart rate.

Finally, it's time for meditation or reading. I enjoy a 10 minute breathing exercise that focuses on the oxygen you take in your body and being grateful. A man is speaking throughout the exercise with a soothing voice reminding you to breathe and as you're breathing to think of 3 things you are grateful for. After your mind is focused on the 3 things you're grateful for, you think of 3 things you are going to accomplish. It can be that day or in the future, but the point is to see yourself already accomplishing it; how do you feel? How does it change your life once completed? You'd be surprised how much energy this creates in your mind.

I first was able to see the benefits at a Tony Robbins event, *Unleash the Power Within*. He takes you on a journey and makes you feel what it would feel like if you didn't achieve what you needed to achieve. He takes you deep into your thought process. This strategy works because if you can feel what it would be like to not achieve what you want, you are definitely more likely to achieve it. Your body will follow what your mind tells it to do. Tony calls it your "state." When your state is off, your day is off. When your state is on, your day is Unstoppable! I had the opportunity to go to the event back in 2018 in Miami. I had always read his books and listened to his podcasts so this was a dream come true for me.

I went by myself and looking back I actually recommend to people to go by yourself. I think if I was with friends or family, I may not have allowed myself to be as vulnerable. If you do go with friends or family, maybe don't sit together. You'll thank me later. It's an experience that allows you to go deep inside your emotions and helps you to discover why you respond the way you do to certain circumstances in your life. It's an on-going journey for me, but I've learned to love and appreciate the process. Writing this book has been very therapeutic for me. You'd be amazed at what comes out of your brain that has been held up for so long. Even if a book is never published, I can see why journaling is so important. You need to release the information. Your brain can only hold so much information and then it either forgets or it's harder to recollect. I'm hopeful my words can help others, but the process has definitely been great for my own wellbeing.

Once I finish my mediation, I'm ready for the day! Mindset is so important. What are you feeding your mind? What are you feeding your body? What are you feeding your spirit? Your answers will define your outcome.

Momentum is an important part of achieving results. Have you ever been on the merry-go-round at the playground? It was the big round wheel that you had to run and hold on until it was moving fast enough to go by itself. Once it was going, you still had to jump down every now and then to build back up to speed. I think of achieving goals as a similar process. Once the momentum is set you must continue to feed it daily to maintain it. Ever wonder why successful people get more successful, the rich get richer, the happy get happier? They've got momentum! This can also work in the negative, be aware of what you are feeding into your life. Daily routines are a key to success. Plan out your month, week, and day to ensure the positive energies are flowing. You are in control of what is around you, make it count.

"Peace is not the absence of conflict, it is the ability to handle conflict by peaceful means."

—Ronald Reagan

CHAPTER 5

Navigating Stormy Waters: Resolving Conflicts with Grace

HAVE YOU EVER WALKED AWAY FROM A SITUATION wishing you would have responded differently?

You've heard the saying, "sticks and stones may break my bones, but words will never hurt me." That cannot be any farther from the truth. Words do hurt. I was in a relationship once where he was physically abusive to me. I've also been in a relationship where I've been talked down to and made to feel like I did not matter. I can honestly tell you the pain of a headbutt goes away much quicker than the pain of words. Fortunately, I'm not in either of these relationships anymore, but I do appreciate what I learned from these experiences.

When faced with conflict, how do you respond? From my

experiences, I've learned to pause. You're completely in control of how you respond. Conflict by definition is a disagreement; a contrast of ideas between two or more people. I've learned to listen, and try to understand their point of view. I think too many times we already have our answers ready before truly listening to what the other person is going to say. It is not about winning or losing. We are put on earth to have relationships, keeping score in a relationship is not a relationship at all, that's a competition. I say save that for the football field!

There are some situations that don't require a response, only an action. For instance, the relationship where I was physically abused: get away and don't look back. There are some people in this world that all you can do is walk away and pray for them. The second step to that sentence is much harder to do, but it is very important for your own wellbeing. If you find yourself in a situation where you are being either physically or mentally abused, please seek help. If you don't have anyone to go to, find me, I will help you. You do matter and no one should ever make you feel any different!

Another book that was life changing for me is *The Four Agreements: A Practical Guide to Personal Freedom* by Don Miguel Ruiz. It really is! I think I'm correct in saying a lot of people struggle with taking things too personally. I've had many interactions throughout my career with young women and men and I think a common trait is being insecure. Insecurity comes from past experiences within or maybe out of your control. Mr. Ruiz talks about how to handle situations by looking through the lens of the other party. When you think about taking things personally, you're basically saying they are responding this way because of you when in most cases their response is from their own past and has nothing to do with you. We see our life through our own eyes, it makes sense until you involve other people. They see life through their own eyes. The book describes it as if you're watching a home movie of yourself and throughout the movie you see how others respond to you. Surprisingly, it's not at all how one would think.

As an example: I come home and I'm acting differently, in my husband's eyes. I'm more quiet than usual, my temperament is more anxious, I'm not acting my usual self. He immediately thinks I'm upset with him. Did she get her hair done and I didn't notice? Did I forget to take out the trash? Did I not respond to a text message? All of these options run through his head. Granted, it's nice that he cares that I am upset, but the truth is it has nothing to do with him: I am missing my children. This scenario could go either way; both of our children live away from us, but the point is still the same. The reason for our actions may have nothing to do with the other person. This leads to another one of the agreements: don't make assumptions. This one will get me into trouble more than not! I think this one has a lot to do with how you deal with conflict. We create a lot of added drama in our lives by making assumptions. It is much better to ask questions than to make assumptions. Assumptions will set you up for suffering. If you've ever watched Saturday Night Live, back in the day, they had a skit that said if you assume, you will make an "Ass out of U and Me." This holds true today.

I had a manager when I worked at Procter and Gamble, he would always say, "I have a fantasy that ......" It was his way of asking you about a situation without anyone getting defensive. He thought it, but made it out like it could just be made up in his mind. Assumptions in our relationships are just asking for trouble. I know I am guilty of wanting my husband to do what I want him to do, but I don't want to tell him because that means he's only doing it because I told him too. I can't even write that without laughing at myself. One thing you have to remember is that all of us are different. We all come from different backgrounds. Ask more questions to get the correct answers instead of assuming them! Keep the communication clear; this will lead to much happier relationships.

When faced with a conflict, I think it's important to see their point of view. Take a moment and pause to ask yourself why they are responding the way they are responding. Take this opportunity to ask more questions. Confirm to yourself that you understand their intentions. Also, does the situation require a response? If you are only wanting to "win" the conversation, sometimes it's best to stay silent. Remembering your response to the conflict is just as important to the situation itself. How you respond is going to affect the outcome, but more importantly how it will affect you. I try to approach each situation with 100% grace and 100% truth. The grace part is very important because it allows you to choose a tone and words that are more likely to be accepted by the person you are conversing with. If you asked some of my earlier relationships they would tell you that I could fight with the best of them, but as I've gotten wiser I no longer put my energy into arguments. I want to save my energy for good. Of course, I still have things that get me upset, but now I have other ways to work through the situations. Both of my sons were in the Navy, my youngest, Troy, is still active. One thing I have learned from both of them is that day-to-day troubles are not worth the energy of getting upset. The things they both have seen and endured makes me appreciate the challenges I may be faced with throughout the day. And if I'm being completely honest, most of my challenges through the day, I've created in my own mind.

"As iron sharpens iron, so one person sharpens another..."
—Proverbs 27:17

CHAPTER 6

Guided by Wisdom: The Role of Mentorship in Your Career

YOU BECOME THE MOST LIKE THE 5 PEOPLE YOU SPEND most of your time with. When I first heard this, I was intrigued. Who do I spend most of my time with? Are they people that I would want to become most like? Who are your 5 people? This made me stop and think about who I choose to spend my time with. You may not have a choice for some. One may be your spouse. If you're younger, it may be your parents or siblings. When you do have the ability to choose, who are your people?

I believe you should choose people who have already achieved what you're trying to achieve. Do not reinvent the wheel. When I worked at Aveda, one of the Directors of Education, Paul, would tell a story of how he became who he was with Aveda. Horst Rechlebacher, the founder of Aveda, still worked behind the chair and Paul wanted to learn all he could from him. Paul made sure that anytime Horst needed something: hair pins, water, shears, or even sweeping the floor, he was there right by his side. He studied his every move. What was his conversation to his clients, how did he hold his shears, how did he stand when cutting hair. Eventually, Horst made him his assistant. He was able to travel to the hair shows with him and take in everything that he did that made him as successful as he was. It worked. Paul created his success. It was intentional. Horst always said, "Learning never ends," and that is how he lived his life. If he wasn't educating, he was being educated. I have so much respect for Horst and the brand of Aveda. His legacy lives on through his brand because he was such a great mentor to others.

Having a mentor in your life allows you the ability to bounce ideas off of someone who has already been there. You trust them because you've seen the results.

Earlier in my career, I worked at Procter and Gamble. I was surrounded by engineers, PHDs, and everyone smarter than me! I worked in research and development for Herbal Essences. I was hired because of my history with Aveda and understanding how to communicate botanicals and fragrance to the consumer. I remember going into one of my first meetings and everyone being on the edge of their seat to hear what I had to say. It was a bit scary. I knew that I was not the smartest person in the room and yet they were interested in what I had to say. This showed me that no matter where you are, there will usually be someone who you can learn from, but they can also learn from you.

My direct report, Andrew, was younger than me. He was an engineer a few years out of college. He was very smart. I remember we clashed quite a bit when I first started, mostly because I needed to be humbled and listen to him. He knew the job and did it very well. I saw on social media that he is now a Director. Well deserved. Had I taken a step back and appreciated the gift that was in front of me, my life may be quite different now. I was surrounded by many different backgrounds and cultures during my time at P&G. I was able to travel to many different countries. I collaborated with design, packaging, legal, advertising, marketing, and research and development during a project. Each day was different in the fact I was interacting with many departments on any given day. I guess my lesson in telling you this is don't take any interaction for granted. Ask questions, listen, and appreciate who is in front of you.

I listen to podcasts when I'm driving in the car. It keeps me motivated. I also buy a lot of self-help books. My son will laugh because I do have some that I have not read yet, but the intention is there. I have always been intrigued with how I can be better. I think that's why the statement you become the most like the 5 people you hang around most resonates with me. I am conscious of who I allow to have my time. If I am going to be the most like someone, it needs to be someone I respect and trust and want their ways to rub off on me. If you are trying to lose weight, are you going to hang out with the person who eats fast food and desserts every day? Probably not. If you want to be an entrepreneur, are you going to spend your time learning from someone who is content working a 9-5? Be intentional with your time. There is one thing that we will never get back and that is your time in the day. Be intentional with who you allow to have your time. If you want to be a millionaire, become friends with a millionaire. Ask questions, take notes, listen to how they speak, walk, and spend their time. Eat where they eat, or if it's possible, ask them out for coffee.

Of all the podcasts I've heard, they all say the same thing when it comes to this topic. Find someone who does what you want to achieve well and study them. Go to the same events they go to. Eat at the same restaurants as they do. Become their friend. Chances are, they were once where you are and would love to help another achieve their dreams.

When I was working as an educator at the Aveda Institute in Nashville, I remember a day the students were learning how to foil hair for a highlight. One student in particular was having such a hard time keeping her foils tight to the scalp. This is very important because otherwise you will have bleeding which can cause a railroad track on the head. Trust me, no one wants that! She tried and tried and was becoming so frustrated. She took herself to a point of being so frustrated, she cried. I took her out into the hall and asked what was wrong. She said, "I can't do it. I will never be able to do it." I remember when I first learned to foil and it was difficult. It is an art to get as close as you can, but not let the product bleed on to the scalp. I told her I understood. I said to her, "If I let you borrow my belief in you, will you promise to give it back once you've achieved how to foil?" She looked at me and seemed confused, but I was very serious. I knew that she did not believe in herself at this moment and belief is what she needed to be successful. I told her, I believe in you. Go back in and do it again. She did and eventually she did it beautifully. Sometimes, all we need is for someone to say out loud, "I believe in you." It can make all the difference.

I love showing people the light that they may not be able to see for themselves. I often wonder why this is so important to me. Why do I love helping others see what they can do? While preparing to write this book, I had a session with one of my mentors and she asked me, "What is your message?" I had never been asked that before. It's a hard question to answer because it means what I have to say others would want to hear. She had me reflect back to my childhood. Who has inspired me? I remembered my 3rd grade teacher, Mrs. Skolaris. I don't remember much of my childhood, but I do remember her. I learned sign language in her class. I can still sign some to this day. I felt good when I was in her class, she was a good teacher and I felt seen and heard with her. She was very attentive to my needs. She was a mentor to me in the way she made me feel about myself. I was never very good with math, I'm so thankful now to have a calculator at my fingertips in my phone. We were learning multiplication; I remember the pages of 1X1, 1X2, 1X3, etc. I dreaded these exercises. But, Mrs. Skolaris was so patient with me. She would go problem by problem, page by page, until I got them right. I will never forget how she made me feel. I hope she is well and had a good teaching career because she was very good at it.

Mentorship can come in many different forms. Having a good mentor also means they will hold you accountable. This is very important. You need to get comfortable being uncomfortable. You will grow the most during uncomfortable times. Your mentor should push you to be better. I was at a church service in Nashville and the pastor said, "Who are your board of directors for your life?" This was very profound. You need a cheerleader, the one who will support and cheer you on no matter what. For me, that's my mom. You need a CFO, the one who will hold you accountable when you are making good or bad financial decisions. You need a QA advisor, one who will audit your behavior and isn't afraid to tell you the truth. Remember 100% Truth + 100% Grace! You are the CEO of your life, you have the ability to spend your time with who you choose. Are you spending your days with those who will make you stronger or those that will keep you complacent? The one thing you will never get back is time…make it count!

Not only should you have a mentor, but I think it's just as important to be a mentor to others. One thing I have learned through educating others is I learn as I'm teaching. Some of the greatest lessons have come while I was at the front of the room. Pay attention to those around you: you can always learn and become better. Remember to allow others to be seen and be heard: you may change their life and not even realize it. My 3rd grade teacher touched my life over 40 years ago and probably never even knew. Be intentional, who knows, you may end up in someone's book.

"The weak can never forgive. Forgiveness is the attribute of the strong."

—*Gandhi*

"Get rid of all bitterness, rage, and anger, harsh words, and slander, as well as all types of malicious behavior. Instead, be kind to each other, tenderhearted, forgiving one another, just as God through Christ has forgiven you."

—*Ephesians* 4:31-32

CHAPTER 7

Graceful Resilience: Harnessing the Power of Forgiveness in Your Life

HOW FRUSTRATING IS IT WHEN SOMEONE WILL TELL you, all you have to do is forgive? That can stir up some emotions in your heart. I don't know your hurt, but I do know my own pain that I have endured throughout my life. Forgiveness is hard, but it is necessary in order to experience freedom in your life.

I like to listen to podcasts as I'm driving and I came across one from Pastor Shawn Johnson. The name was *When Past Hurts, Still Hurt*. I was intrigued. I've been hurt in the past, maybe it's worth listening to. It was very powerful and well worth my time.

I'm not here to say my hurt is worse than anyone else's, but I am here to say that my hurt was painful to me. It was a pain that I had to come to terms with because it was defining me and driving me to make decisions that I may otherwise not have made.

We moved to Cincinnati when I was 11 years old. It was my mom, dad, me, and my brother. We didn't know anyone so we spent a lot of time together. We were what you would call a "game" family. My dad was always coming up with games to play. I remember when we got our first camcorder, he would create game shows with us and our friends. He also made music videos with characters we had around the house. There was never a dull moment, but one thing I remember is we were always together. On Christmas, because we didn't have family close by to visit, we would go to the movies to see the latest release. One year it was Rocky IV! My brother played sports and we were always there to watch and cheer him on. We ate dinner together at the dinner table almost every night. Our friends were always welcome. Our house was fun! It always felt like a home.

One night after a high school dance, Johnny and I came home and heard Mom and Dad in their bedroom having an argument. One thing my parents did well is hide their arguments from us. Looking back, I'm not sure if that is a good thing or not, but all I can say is I remember the feeling I had that night like it was yesterday. My mom told my dad she wanted a divorce. Johnny and I were standing in the hallway and just looked at each other. I remember there was not a feeling of, "oh, this will pass," we knew it was real. I was a sophomore and Johnny was a senior. It was February and we had just come from the King of Hearts Dance. We had just finished the football season where the team had won the State Championship and Mom and Dad were at every game. Dad would video every game and make highlight videos for Johnny. Mom and I would have our faces painted with little Indians from Dad. Even some of my friends would come over before the game for my Dad to paint their faces. Times were good. We were a happy family. Or so I thought.

Evidently, Mom and Dad were not happy for quite some time. They decided to wait until Johnny finished high school before separating and getting a divorce. Johnny got a full ride football scholarship to Eastern Michigan University. They wanted to make sure that went smoothly for him.

Within 1 year, my parents split and my brother moved away. Needless to say, it rocked my world. I carried on with the day-to-day because that's what you do, but it changed something inside of me that I wouldn't realize until much later in life. I don't blame anyone, but your circumstances around you do have an affect on you whether you realize it in the moment or later in life. I take that back, I did lay blame for a lot of years, and I'm past that now, but it was a process.

At the time I was in a relationship with my high school boyfriend. What I didn't know then was that subconsciously I was going to make sure no one would ever leave me again. I actually sabotaged the relationship to where there was nothing else to do but break up. In my mind, I lost my family, my Mom (who moved to Memphis), and my brother, and I was not going to let anyone else bring me pain by leaving me. I was the one to decide; therefore, I broke up with him. It broke my heart, but I was able to convince myself that it was better than me being hurt by him leaving me. I felt everyone I loved and counted on had left me. Granted, my Mom wanted me to move to Memphis with her, but I was in high school. I wasn't going to leave my friends, my boyfriend, or my home. I lived with my Dad. He traveled for work, which left me home by myself a lot. My parents did what they needed to do for their lives. We moved out of our home and from condo to condo each year because he just rented. My brother would come home to visit and we would go to watch him play football at college. It was never the same. Our family, as I once knew it, was no more.

As I reflect back on all of my relationships, I have always been the one to decide when it is over. I was in counseling for many years with my Pastor and he described it as I was sitting in a chair and I was surrounded by boxes. I would move them a little to see through and maybe let you see me, but as soon as I feel vulnerable, I push the boxes back and block anyone from getting close to me. I did this for many years. It was my protection from being hurt. But, I also held back from loving others and allowing others to love me.

Back to the podcast I mentioned earlier, Pastor Shawn Johnson says the first step to forgiveness is acknowledging the hurt. You cannot minimize the effects it has on you. You must face it, and feel it in order to forgive it. I was mad at my mom and dad for many years for getting a divorce. I know that sounds like a silly kid pouting as I say it, but it was real to me. Going deep into the feelings of how it made me feel; the pain, the sadness, the feeling of being alone, and abandoned. It takes a lot of energy to hold on to the unforgiveness in your heart. The decisions that you make come from that place of hurt. You are protecting yourself without even realizing it. But, at the same time what are you protecting yourself from?

I got pregnant with my daughter, Chelsey, at 19 years old. I married her father because I was pregnant and felt it was the right thing to do. I know now I did not love him. He was the sabotage that broke up me and my highschool boyfriend. I was careless, but God gave me a blessing: my daughter. Chelsey was my saving grace. She was my reason to live and thrive.

The relationship between me and her father didn't last long. The day I told him I was leaving I was in the bathtub with Chelsey, who was about 3 months old. He came in and grabbed me by my bangs and slammed my head into the back of the bathtub. This was not the first time he had done something like this. It seemed anytime he felt threatened, he would try to show his authority and head butt me. Fortunately, I left after the bathtub incident. For many years after, we would go back and forth to court fighting over custody of Chelsey. I'll spare you the gory details, but needless to say, I carried a lot of hate for him for many years. In order to forgive, you must acknowledge the pain. I have gone back to each and every incident with him in order to face it, feel it, and ultimately forgive him. Unforgiveness will harden your heart if you allow it to go on for too long. The need to forgive is not about them, it's about you. Holding on to unforgiveness will harden your heart and eventually block you from feeling anything good. Understanding that it is a process is important. It's not like flipping a switch.

I want to take a moment to talk about what forgiveness is and what it is not. It's very important to understand. Forgiveness is freedom for YOU! Forgiveness is not justifying their actions. Forgiveness is not a guarantee you will be back in my life. It is important to know the difference. Just because I forgive you that doesn't mean it's a good thing for us to be in each other's lives. My forgiveness is for my heart, to be clear.

Chelsey is now pregnant with my first grandchild! We had her gender reveal party a couple of months ago. I made a point to let Chelsey know that I was ok with her father being at the party. This was the first time I felt completely content with being around him. I forgive him, but we will still spend our lives at a distance.

Forgiveness is a process. If you truly want to forgive, you must also give up your right to punish the person for their wrong doing. Romans 12:19 says, "I will take vengeance; I will repay those who deserve it, says the Lord." It is not up to us to punish or judge others. If you are going to forgive someone it means you cannot hold it over their head. For example: a husband and wife have an argument and all is "forgiven," but the next time they have an argument someone brings it up again or says, "I remember when…." You cannot use it as leverage against the other party. If you are truly trying to forgive then you must let it go! I know I have been guilty of this a time or two, but I recognize the importance. You cannot use it as a way of controlling the other party. That is manipulation, not love.

One of the hardest parts of forgiveness for me is to pray for them.

Matthew 5:44 says: "But, I say, love your enemies! Pray for those who hurt you!" Forgiveness is a process, this is the biggest step towards your own personal freedom. I pray for Chelsey's father every night. He has never apologized to me, in fact he has never admitted anything he did to me. As I said earlier, forgiveness is for you not for the other party. I can let go because I need my heart to be healed. I was upset for many years because I thought I needed him to admit it. But, why? I know it happened and I know the pain it caused me. All I needed was for my heart to be healed. Forgiveness gave me that.

Back to the story of my parents. They both have apologized to me. Not for getting a divorce, but for the way it happened. They purposefully waited for Johnny to finish high school, not taking into account that I still had 2 years left and how it would affect my life. They probably wouldn't have changed when it happened, but I do believe they are sincere about not wanting me to hurt and feel the way that I did. An apology is not just saying "I'm sorry." An apology is true repentance. Repentance is admitting you were wrong, saying I'm sorry, asking for forgiveness, and changing your ways to make sure it does not happen again. Have you ever had someone say to you: "I'm sorry..if that hurt you," or, "I'm sorry..if you misunderstood what I meant," or, "I'm sorry..if you took it that way." These are not apologies, these are excuses and justifications. Actions speak louder than words! Their actions will show you if they deserve to be in your life. Be true to yourself and do not allow this behavior. You deserve to be respected.

To give you the ending of the story, with the help of Jesus, I found my true love. Someone that I have taken down the boxes for and allowed him to see all of me. I could only do it once I was ready and I had the ability to forgive and open my heart to freedom. For the first time in my life, I don't have to be the first to leave. I don't want to run away. I know in my heart I am healed and I will be just fine. Thank you, Jesus!

Forgiveness is for YOU! Forgiveness is a process! Forgiveness will set you FREE!

"Work like you don't have a family & Mother like you don't work."

—*Frances Katzen*

CHAPTER 8

Balancing Act: Parenting While Thriving in Your Career

RAISING CHILDREN WHILE MAINTAINING A CAREER IS challenging, especially if you find yourself in a split family. Most of my career, I was a single mom. Juggling the kids' school, events, after school activities, and getting to work on time. I did not want to be the mom who missed their children's events, and I was fortunate enough that I was able to attend most of them. I have been a mom more of my life than not being a mom. I love being a mom. One of my best memories is when me and the kids had a house in Trenton, Ohio on Hamilton Trenton Rd. It was just the 4 of us. I couldn't afford cable, so we watched VHS movies or played video games. I took from my parents the fun of playing games. We are definitely a "game" family.

Uno, Catch Phrase, Monopoly, Clue, and many others. I will always cherish our game times.

Chelsey cheered and the boys played football, basketball, and baseball. Our days, nights, and weekends were filled with activities. I would not have changed it for the world. At the time, I worked at Procter and Gamble which was a 40 hour a week job. I left in the morning after getting the kids off to school and tried to be home close to when they got home. They were old enough to be alone for a bit, but I liked to be there with them. We had dinner together unless we were running from practice to practice and then I tried to make something to take with us. I tried not to do too much fast food. It's not good for them, but also I was on a tight budget.

This calls for a moment of advice to anyone who is getting a divorce with children and thinks they can do it on their own without child support - don't do it! I chose this because I didn't want to cause controversy between me and the boys' dad (at this point, you have probably figured out Chelsey and the boys have a different Dad). He would help out if I asked, but the court knows what they are doing when they set up a steady income for the parent who has the children. It helps to pay for daily expenses. This is one thing I would've changed for sure!

On the other hand, my children knew how to enjoy life without all the bells and whistles. I am proud to say all 3 of them are good with money as adults. They appreciate what they have and that in and of itself is priceless! I remember a time when our electricity had been shut off because I was late on the payment. I set up a blanket in the living room, lit some candles and we had goldfish crackers and played UNO. The kids thought we were having a picnic. They had no idea the electricity had been turned off. They still speak of that today as being one of the "coolest" times together.

As a working parent, it's important to think quality versus quantity while also keeping in mind you will not get the time back. What do you remember about your childhood? Were your parents present? Now, as they are adults, we all live in different parts of the country. Florida, Ohio, Tennessee, and Washington. Our times together are precious, short and sweet! Thank goodness for technology. I love that I can Facetime. Even though they don't always like it, they will answer, eventually.

I go back to my brother when I think about a working parent juggling time with family and work. He is the Executive Vice President of Colosseum Athletics. He oversees the sales team nationwide. He lives in Nashville, the corporate office is in California, and he travels the nation to support his team in addition to events that happen throughout the year. Johnny and his wife, Karen, have 3 boys who have all been very involved in sports since a very young age. Johnny has made sure to be available to coach all 3 boys in various sports and does not miss a game! All while being a loving husband to his wife of 30 years! He does not do it alone, obviously this is an example of a married couple raising their children together. I truly honor the family they have created together.

It's important for children to see you work hard, but it's just as important for them to feel seen, heard, and know that you are a part of their everyday life. The world we live in can take over your time if you allow it to.

Having a detailed plan is important. Setting aside time for a monthly, or even weekly brain dump is essential. A brain dump is taking out a piece of paper and dumping everything from your brain into words. What do you have to do today, tomorrow, or next week? Then, prioritizing the important versus urgent. Stop and think about this: important versus urgent. There is a difference. Important are the things that need to be done, but you may have some time to complete them. Urgent are the time sensitive items. I don't like the term time management because I think it's been overused, but the idea of it holds true. People say they don't have enough time, but we all have the same amount of time. It's what we choose to do with the time we are given during the day. Time is not the problem, we are the problem.

What are you doing with your time? How much time do you spend on your phone? How much time do you watch TV? How much time do you spend on social media or Netflix? Technology has given us many more options of what we choose to do with our time. The ability to be more efficient is at your fingertips. We all operate in the same 24/7 hours. It's how you prioritize your 24/7 hours.

I like to keep a paper calendar, as well as I put my appointments into my phone in order to get the "ding" when I'm getting close to the time of my appointment. I also keep a running list of things that need to be done on any given day. During my "brain dump" I will pull out the priorities that need to be done each week and then single it down to per day. You can take it even further and take it hour by hour. I'm not that detailed, although I do see the benefits. I love to check off my list throughout the day. You've heard of dopamine, the spark of energy you receive when you're stimulated in your brain. I get my dopamine charge each time I'm able to check a task off of my list. Try it!

Your children will grow up - time doesn't stop that either. I am truly blessed to have 3 children who are successful and happy in their lives. They also respect me and know I did the best I could to give them a great childhood. I made some mistakes, as we all do, but not a moment goes by that I ever question if they know how much they mean to me. We all live separately now, but thank goodness for FaceTime. We have a joint call together as often as we can and I will cherish those moments forever! Until we can all be together in the same room again - which hopefully is very soon! My children have helped to make me who I am today. I love them very much!

Chelsey is married to her high school sweetheart, Dakota. They are having their first child, Mackenzie, my first grandchild. They live in Ohio and are doing fantastic! Dakota is a part of the family. He's been around as long as I can remember at this point. He is so very good to Chelsey and that is all I could ever ask for. They have a dog, Clyde and a cat, Nala. Jake is living in Knoxville finishing his college career and working at a gym. His passion is working out and helping others to achieve their workout goals. Jake has a dog, Charlie. Troy is in Washington State in the Navy. He is married to Gabriella. They have 2 cats, Winston and Edgar and a dog, Alikai which keeps them busy. I miss my children so much.

Our time together is what I cherish the most in life. We all went to Hawaii a couple years ago to visit Troy while he was stationed in Pearl Harbor. It was just the 4 of us, like old times. One night, we were in the hotel and I just lied there and watched them all play video games. Laughing and carrying on like they were teenagers again. I went sky-diving with Jake and Troy; checked that off my bucket list. Memories are what life is all about. Don't miss this. Take the trip. I don't ever want to think back and wish I would've done more. I work to have freedom. Freedom to go and see my children and soon to be granddaughter whenever I want. Freedom to take trips with them. Freedom to make more memories.

"A one hour workout is
4% of your day,
no excuses."
—Unknown

"Life has its ups and downs, we call them squats."

—*Unknown*

CHAPTER 9

Nurturing Self: Balancing Self-Health in a Demanding Career

YOUR BODY WILL FOLLOW WHAT YOUR MIND BEGINS. If you can motivate your mind, your body will follow through. I never have thought of myself as an athlete. I didn't play sports throughout school. I was always the last one picked in gym class. Once I began CrossFit it was like a light turned on inside of me. I had this whole new world of competing that I did not know was even possible in my mind. I'm not competing with anyone but myself. How much faster will I finish tomorrow, how many wall balls will I do, how many burpees can I withstand? To me, there is no greater feeling than walking out of the gym knowing I accomplished the WOD! CrossFit may not be for everyone, but the process your mind and body go through can be applied to other parts of your life. If I can get my body to climb a rope, I can do anything!

Kobe Bryant said, "Great things come from hard work and perseverance. NO Excuses."

You will never get to where you want to be if you're not willing to put in the work. What are you willing to go through to achieve the results you desire? Discipline is not meant to be easy, but the regret you will feel if you do not achieve your desired results, I feel is much worse. I have seen changes in my body that I didn't think were possible, especially in my 50s. It's dedication and discipline. If I miss a workout, I feel it. I have trained my mind and my body that working out is now the norm. I have trained my mind and body that eating right is now the norm. Just as your mind and body can get used to the bad, it can also get used to the good! The choice is yours, there is no right or wrong, this has been my choice.

I see some of my loved ones who struggle with ailments in their life. A lot of which, I believe, are due to habits throughout their life: smoking, not eating right, lack of exercise. If God allows me to live a long life, I want that life to be full of excitement where I'm not limited on what I can do and where I can go because of my health. As I write this, I realize I am opening up my life to accountability from everyone who reads my book. I did that on purpose! On the mornings when I don't "feel" like getting up, I will because I won't let you down. More importantly, I won't let myself down.

Stress and worry can take its toll on your life. You can see someone who is 50, but they look like they're 30 or someone who is 30, looks like they are 50. Stress, worry, anxiety, the sun, not enough sleep, being angry, and holding on to unforgiveness will make a difference in how your body ages. More peace in your life means the slower you age. The more frustration in your life, the faster you will age. Life can and will be challenging, but being prepared and knowing how you will allow yourself to handle challenging situations is very important.

I used to stress over the craziest things, my children will attest to this. When putting away the dishes, I would get so upset if the big spoons were put in the same space as the little spoons. I allowed this to drive me crazy! Folding towels was another thing I obsessed about. There was a right way and a wrong way to fold a towel. Or at least that's what I told myself. Now, I'm happy to have someone help me with the laundry. I was in control of how I allowed these things to affect me. It took me a long time to realize big spoon, little spoon, it doesn't matter! Don't sweat the small stuff. Life is too short. Be aware of the stress you may be creating in your mind. Is it worth it? Does it really matter?

You need to have people in your life who will hold you accountable. I spoke of the theory that you are most like the 5 people you hang around. Who are your 5 people? Do they have similar goals? Do they exercise? Are they concerned with their health? You need people that will lovingly push you to your end result.

My son, Jake, moved to Florida for a brief time. I loved having him close for many reasons, but one in particular: he called me out on my lifestyle. During COVID I had started drinking more than I had in the past, in fact I would have at least one drink everyday. If I'm being honest, it was more than one each day. Living in Florida, we were only locked down for a few months, but during that time it was easy to have a drink around 3:00. What else were you to do? Once the lockdown was lifted, my habit didn't change. One of my worst memories is talking to my children and them saying, "Mom we talked about this last night, don't you remember talking to me?" I didn't remember. I drank too much. Time was lost. I was mortified. What I realized is when I would drink everyday my body picked up where it left off from the night before. When I would only have 1 drink, my body felt like it was my 3rd or 4th drink. This was awful. What was I doing to my body? In the moment, you don't realize it, or you don't want to. I was having fun, but what was I doing to my body and what were the long term implications?

Jake called me out. I went to work everyday, but went out drinking every night. I had gained weight, I was tired, I was not who my son knew me to be. Things had to change.

We live on an island where most are retired. They have worked very hard to be where they are today. They have savings that allows them to relax and live the life they worked very hard for most of their lives. I am not retired, in fact I began a new career just 4 short years ago! I need to be on the top of my game. I still have a lot of work to do. I needed to make a change.

If you know Jake, you know he is very aware of his health and physical fitness. He has always been one to eat right and work out. This was the perfect accountability partner for me. If you ever want to change a bad habit, make a promise to someone that you love and you will not let them down.

Whole 30 is a diet that was introduced to me through the CrossFit gym that I attend. I really like this plan. During a 30 day period you eliminate alcohol, sugar, dairy, wheat, beans, and pasta from your diet. I became very aware of my body and how certain foods can affect me and how I feel. What I realized is the dairy was causing inflammation in my body. It made me feel bloated. I have always loved cheese, but I have trained my mind and body that I can only have it in moderation. It has made a huge difference in how I feel day-to-day. Also, my bathroom time is much better! The first time I did Whole30, I lost 12 pounds. Intermittent fasting has also been successful for me. It's not for everyone, but I think it helps my digestive system.

I was with eXp Realty for a short time, but was fortunate enough to meet some very influential people. Through a connection I had made, I was able to be a part of a study with Stanford University. It was a year-long study involving Tony Robbins. They were testing how your body reacts, psychologically and physically, to his events. We were able to attend each event throughout the year virtually, and had to answer questionnaires of how we were feeling during certain times of the event as well as after the event. Now, if you know me at all you know I love Tony Robbins! I was able to attend: *Date with Destiny*, *Unleash the Power Within*, and *Business Mastery*. I was also on a chat with over 100 people worldwide who were also doing the study with me. We would often ask each other questions about anything going on in our lives. There were several doctors involved in the study too. One of the doctors was talking about intermittent fasting and it made so much sense to me. He said that just like your body needs sleep to rejuvenate itself, your stomach needs a break to digest the food that you've put in your body. I also like to throw in a 24 hour fast now and then. Everyone is different. Your body will tell you what works and what doesn't. I know I feel fantastic since changing my ways. Find what works and stick to it.

> "Success is the sum of small efforts - repeated day in and day out."
> —Robert Collier

Darren Hardy's book, *The Compound Effect*, speaks to making little changes each day and how it can affect your end result.

It's the small wins that lead you to the big win.

Let's say you're living life without a thought of death and the Angel of Death comes to you and says, "come, it's time to go." You say, "no. You're supposed to give me a warning so I can decide what to do with my last week." He says, "I gave you 52 weeks this past year alone and look at all of the other weeks you've had, what did you do with them?""

—Michael A. Singer,
from *The Untethered Soul*

"Failure is success in progress."
—Albert Einstein

"Make sure your worst enemy doesn't live between your own two ears."

—*Laird Hamilton*

CHAPTER 10

Celebrating Success: Recognizing and Leveraging Your Wins

ARE YOU LIVING YOUR LIFE FULLY WITHOUT COMPROMISE? What have been your biggest wins? What are you most proud of? How do you define success? What is your legacy? What do people say about you when you're not in the room?

Success: the accomplishment of an aim or purpose. What are you aiming for? Are you on the right track to achieve it? Success comes in many forms and can be very different for everyone. A lot depends on your core values and the goals you have set for yourself. Understanding your core values and your "blueprint," as John Maxwell describes it, is very important. If you don't know what you're striving for, how will you know once you've reached it? What is important to you? Why?

How would you feel if you didn't achieve it? How would it impact your life? How would it impact those you love?

Determining your core values is a practice you must complete before truly understanding your goals. You need to know what you're striving for, but also why? If you are not aligning your goals with your why, you will not have the power and focus to maintain the course. Your blueprint is your core beliefs. Your core beliefs are determined at a very young age. Your core beliefs often determine your behavior and how you react to things happening in your life. How you respond to circumstances without thought are usually aligned with your core values. There are many ways to identify your core values.

1. You could write down a list of values and circle the ones that resonate the most with you. Continue to redefine the list until you have your top 5.
2. Reflect on past experiences. Consider both positive and negative experiences from your past and present and identify common themes. You could consider situations that made you happy, sad, angry, proud, energized, fulfilled, and satisfied. Think of a painful moment in your life, what did you learn from it? Empathy or how to be compassionate towards others? Maybe a time when you won an award for teaching, it's possible that motivating others and leadership are important to you.
3. Who do you admire? Who are your heroes? What are their values that you find appealing? What draws you to them? How do you feel when you are around them?

I had a mentor early in my career, Julie. She was electrifying. Her positivity was contagious. I loved being around her. She was my partner while servicing the salons in Ohio and she was so knowledgeable on the products, the services, and how to engage with the salon owners in a way that they hung on every word she spoke. I loved going to salons with her. I would watch her every move. The way she interacted with the staff was like they had been friends for years. She could really work a room. She was authentic and true. I would reach out to her often during my time at Aveda. I trusted her and was always willing to obtain feedback from her on how I could improve myself, personally and in my career. She has never let me down.

One of my heroes is Princess Diana. She was beautiful on the inside and out. She loved her children with her whole heart. She donated her time and energy towards helping others, especially children. She went through a painful time, but endured and always handled herself with the utmost grace. She was taken from this world too soon, I believe, but God had a plan and there was a reason, one that I am not to question. If I could sit down for lunch (or tea) with anyone, my choice would be Princess Diana. I would be intrigued to hear her stories of her travels to other countries to help those in need. My bucket list is getting shorter as my life goes on, but one thing I long to do is a missionary trip. To be able to give my time and energy to those in need would be a dream come true.

Knowing your core values will help you to define your purpose. What do you want out of your life? It helps to guide your behavior. When you are acting out of line of your core values, you feel off. It hinders what you are capable of achieving. Identifying your values brings a sense of safety and stability into your life, a sense of confidence because you know what you want and what's important to you.

Once you've established your core values, you can set goals. We've all heard, "you have to set goals," but have you really sat down and written out what you want to achieve in the next month, year, or 5 years? Something you want to accomplish that is not written down is not a goal, it's just an idea. A goal is something that has a realistic time period attached to it. You need to have an end in sight in order to have a set time to achieve such a goal. A goal must also be specific. "I want to lose some weight." Ok, great, is 1 pound enough? "I want to lose 15 pounds over the next 3 months." Now we're getting somewhere. A goal must also have an action plan. How are you going to achieve such a goal? "I want to lose 15 pounds over the next 3 months. I will go to the gym at least 3 times a week, no sugar, drink more water, and hire a trainer to help me." Your goal must also be realistic. It is not healthy to lose 15 pounds in 1 week, but it is healthy and reasonable to lose 15 pounds in 3 months through diet and exercise. An easy way to remember to include all of the steps when setting a goal is to use the acronym, "SMART". S=Specific, M=Measurable, A=Actionable, R=Realistic, and T=Timebound. Write your goal down and put it where you can see it each day. Maybe on your bathroom mirror or refrigerator. If your goal has to do with weight, I recommend your refrigerator: you may think twice before going in for a late night snack.

I feel it's important to celebrate your wins, even the small ones. This is one reason I like to make a list of the things I need to accomplish on any given day: I get to check off the list when I've completed my task! Winning!

Track your personal wins somewhere you can see it daily. This will give you the momentum to continue to push to the next level. If it's where others can see it, it will help to hold you accountable. I know this works wonders for me. The more people I tell my goals to, the more apt I am to achieve them. I do not like to let myself down, but definitely don't want to let others down.

Find an accountability partner. Share your goals with each other and check in once a week or once a month. It's easier to do the harder things in life with a partner to share through the struggles and celebrations. I like CrossFit because I have a group that I work out with each day. We celebrate our personal bests with one another. As long as you have someone to share it with, your mind will continue to push yourself to achieve it.

I'm going to end this book with several quotes and phrases that

I have looked at throughout my life that have helped to keep me on track. I hope they will help you too!

Thank you for reading my book.

"There is only one way to eat an elephant, one bite at a time."
—Desmond Tutu

"Buy the front row to meet the front row people."
—Rene Rodriguez

"Be the Mayor of your Mile."
—Luca Boccia

"Be comfortable being in the room, when you're not yet in the room."
—Dina Godentayer

"Ready, Fire, Aim."
—Josh Altman

"Describe me without using my name."
—Ryan Serhant

"Act like the person you want to be in 2 years."
—*Ryan Serhant*

"In the "no" comes the opportunity to grow."
—*Julie Mullins*

"Make sure the people in your life are making more deposits than withdrawals."
—*Unknown*

"Don't wish it was easier, wish you were better. Don't wish for less problems, wish for more skills. Don't wish for less challenge, wish for more wisdom."
—Jim Rohn

"There are no shortcuts to any place worth going."
—John Maxwell

"Change is inevitable. Growth is optional."
—Joyce Meyer

"A bird sitting on a tree is never afraid
of the branch breaking, because her
trust is not on the branch,
but on its own wings. Always
believe in yourself."
—*Unknown*

"Today is the first day of the
rest of your life."
—*Jack Nightwine*
(Grandpa)

ACKNOWLEDGMENTS

The Rising Tides Foundation
The Rising Tides Foundation is a cause close to my heart. I founded it three years ago alongside two of my closest friends, Al Beltran and Georgette Angelos, with the mission of raising funds to give back to our local community. It has been an honor to serve as the President of this foundation and witness the impact we've made together.

Photography Credit

A special thank you to **ipixx**, the talented photographer who took my picture for the cover photo. Your work captured this moment in time beautifully, and I truly appreciate your contribution.

Additionally, thank you to **JoLee Art and Photography** for capturing the professional photo on the back cover. Your creativity and skill are greatly appreciated.

Gemstone Title & Real Estate of Florida

As a part-owner of Gemstone Title & Real Estate of Florida, I am proud to be part of a company dedicated to excellence in the real estate industry. Thank you to my partners and team for your support throughout this journey.

Colosseum Athletics

The outfit I am wearing on the front cover is made by Colosseum Athletics—a brand that embodies strength and resilience. I appreciate their craftsmanship and dedication to quality.

To everyone who has supported me along the way, from my closest friends and family to the incredible teams I work with, thank you. This journey would not have been possible without you.

www.ingramcontent.com/pod-product-compliance
Lightning Source LLC
Chambersburg PA
CBHW050917160426
43194CB00011B/2448